D1410038

Out and About at the PUBLIC LIBRARY

by Kitty Shea

illustrated by Zachary Trover

PICTURE WINDOW BOOKS
Minneapolis, Minnesota

Special thanks to our advisers for their expertise:

Ronelle Thompson, Director, Mikkelsen Library
Augustana College, Sioux Falls, South Dakota

Susan Kesselring, M.A., Literacy Educator
Rosemount–Apple Valley–Eagan (Minnesota) School District

The author wishes to thank Holly Rakocy, Bill Erickson, and Nancy Hirdler of the Westonka Community Library in Mound, Minnesota, for their behind-the-stacks tour.

Editorial Director: Carol Jones
Managing Editor: Catherine Neitge
Creative Director: Keith Griffin
Editor: Jill Kalz
Story Consultant: Terry Flaherty
Designer: Zachary Trover
Page Production: Picture Window Books
The illustrations in this book were created digitally.

Picture Window Books
5115 Excelsior Boulevard
Suite 232
Minneapolis, MN 55416
877-845-8392
www.picturewindowbooks.com

Printed in the United States of America.

Library of Congress Cataloging-in-Publication Data
Shea, Kitty.
Out and about at the public library / by Kitty Shea ; illustrated by Zachary Trover.
p. cm. — (Field trips)
Includes bibliographical references and index.
ISBN 1-4048-1150-8 (hardcover)
1. Public libraries—Juvenile literature. 2. Library orientation for school children.
I. Trover, Zachary. II. Title. III. Field trips (Picture Window Books)
Z665.5.S54 2005
027.4—dc22
2005004266

We're going on a field trip to the library. We can't wait!

Things to find out:

What's at the library besides books?

Can librarians answer every question we have?

How do we check things out?

What happens to books after they go through the Returns slot?

MATH IS FUN!

Welcome to West Ridge Public Library! My name is Howard, and I'm a librarian. There is so much to do and so much to check out at the library.

We have books, magazines, videotapes, and even DVDs.

Today, I'll show you how to find and check out a book. Please remember that people come to the library to read and study, so use your indoor voices.

The United States has more than 117,000 libraries. Public libraries are open to anyone. School libraries serve students and teachers. Research libraries have information that doctors, scientists, or other professionals need for their jobs.

RETURNS

Rea
Spook

At the library, you can borrow books and materials for free, as long as you bring them back to share with others. Reference books stay in the library for everyone to use. So, if you need a dictionary or encyclopedia, they are always here. Some reference materials are also available on computers.

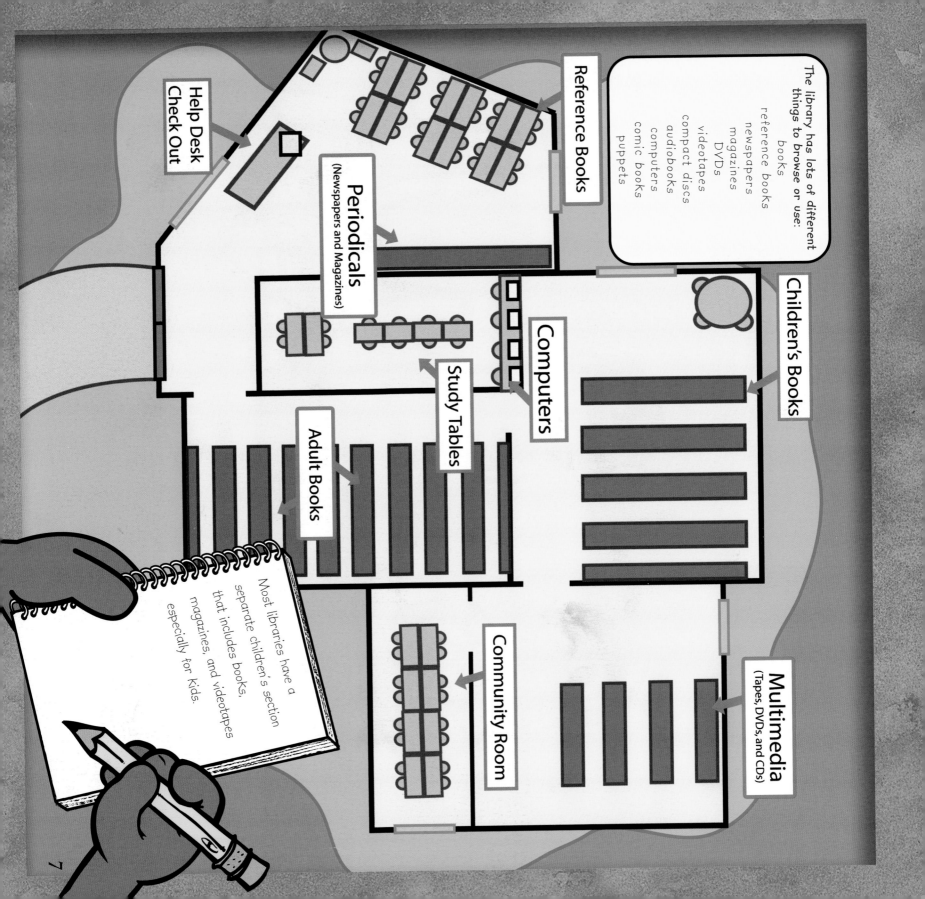

Librarians get asked lots of questions: "What do goldfish eat?" "Is Sunday the first day of the week, or is Monday?" "What's the tallest mountain in the world, and where is it?"

INFORMATION

You might think librarians are super smart and know all the answers. The truth is, we don't know all the answers, but we know where to find them. We can show you where to find the answers you need.

Don't Forget To Read!

Books Are Good!

READ!

To become a librarian, you must first complete four years of college and then study library science for another year or two. It's called a science because all libraries are set up and run the same basic way.

If it's in the library, it's in our library catalog. Let's say you're looking for a special book. If you know the title or author, the computer can tell you if we have it and where to find it. If all you know is that the book is about zebras, type in the subject "zebras."

If your library doesn't have the book you want, you can borrow it from another library. This is called interlibrary loan. Libraries work together to make sure people have all the materials they need.

Each library book has its own call number. A call number is the book's address. It is made up of numbers and letters. The call number tells you where the book lives on our shelves. The computer said that the zebra book should be right about ... here!

Many libraries put books in order using the Dewey Decimal System. This system groups books by subject.

000 General Works
100 Philosophy and Psychology
200 Religion
300 Social Sciences
400 Language
500 Natural Sciences
600 Technology
700 Arts
800 Literature
900 Geography and History

13

All you need to check out library materials is a library card. Nancy scans the bar code on your library card and the bar codes on your selections. A bar code is a row of thin lines that tells the computer your name and the titles of the materials you checked out.

Be sure to handle library materials with care.

• Wash your hands before opening a book. Peanut butter or bike grease make pages stick together.

• Use a bookmark to mark your place in books.

• Carry items to and from the library in a waterproof bag or backpack to keep them dry and clean.

Reading Makes you Smarter!

15

You can keep books from this library for three weeks. Videos and DVDs are checked out for one week. Then they are due back.

16

Returning things to the library is fun! You get to drop them through the Returns slot. Then library workers check them in and put the materials back on our shelves for someone else to check out.

Something is overdue if it's not returned by its due date. At many libraries, you pay a fine for each day it's late. Libraries charge fines to help users remember to return things they borrow.

17

Library cards are free. All you have to do to get one is write your name and address on this form. You can each get a card today before you leave!

READ A BOOK!

Bring your library card
along every time you come
to the library so you can
check things out.

WEST RIDGE
PUBLIC LIBRARY

Expires 06/09

SIGNATURE

WEST RIDGE PUBLIC LIBRARY

Librarians say that among the library books that are read over and over again are *A Christmas Carol* by Charles Dickens, the *Harry Potter* series by J. K. Rowling, the *Little House on the Prairie* series by Laura Ingalls Wilder, and *Winnie the Pooh* by A. A. Milne.

Thanks for stopping in today. Come browse our shelves anytime. Bring a friend with you—or even your mom and dad! The West Ridge Public Library is here for everyone!

MAKING YOUR OWN LIBRARY

Now that you know how a library works, gather some books and make your own library!

What you need:

books
a pencil
note cards
sheets of paper
tape
large boxes
a current calendar

What you do:

1. Print the title of each book on the top of two note cards. Print the author's name below it. Under this information, make two columns, and label them "Name" and "Due Date."

2. Tuck the two cards into the middle of each book so their edges stick out the top when the book is closed.

3. Sort the books into piles based on what they are about. You might have one pile for story books, another pile for craft books, and a pile for books about everything else. Try to make sure each pile has at least three books.

4. Make a sign for each pile on a sheet of paper. One sign might say "Stories," another "Crafts," and the third "Everything Else."

5. The boxes are your library's bookshelves. Each subject gets a bookshelf of its own. Arrange the books in each pile into alphabetical order by author last name. Tape the correct sign to each box so visitors know where to find books about that subject.

6. Invite your family and friends to visit your library. To check out a book, they must take out the note cards and write their names on both of them.

7. Look at the calendar. Count out two weeks and write that date (the due date) on both of the note cards. Keep one note card for the library. Tuck the other one back in the book.

8. When books are returned, tuck the second note card back into the book and put it back on the correct shelf.

FUN FACTS

- Famous inventor Benjamin Franklin helped set up the first public library in the United States. His Library Company of Philadelphia opened in 1731.

- Mobile libraries serve areas that don't have actual libraries. Bookmobiles can be small trucks or big, fancy buses outfitted with bookshelves, computer stations, and children's corners. Bookboats deliver books by river and sea. There are also book bikes in Chile, camel-drawn libraries in Kenya, and donkey libraries in Zimbabwe.

- The Library of Congress in Washington, D.C., is the national library of the United States. It is the largest library in the world. It has 530 miles (850 kilometers) of bookshelves filled with more than 29 million books and other printed materials. Approximately 7,000 new materials are added each workday.

- The biggest book in the Library of Congress is as tall as the average 3-year-old child. *Birds of America* by John James Audubon is 39.4 inches (100 centimeters) high and contains life-size drawings of birds.

GLOSSARY

author—a person who writes a book

browse—to look at

dictionary—a book that lists words in alphabetical order and tells how to say them and what they mean

encyclopedia—a book that gives information on subjects that are usually arranged in alphabetical order

fine—a small amount of money that libraries charge when items aren't returned on time

librarian—a person who is trained in library science and helps library visitors

library catalog—a list of a library's books and materials; listings usually include title, author, subject, call number, and the year published or released

reference books—books that contain information useful to many people

TO LEARN MORE

At the Library

Greene, Carol. *At the Library*. Chanhassen, Minn.: Child's World, 1999.

Kottke, Jan. *A Day with a Librarian*. New York: Children's Press, 2000.

Lee, Carol K., and Janet Langford. *Learning About Books and Libraries: A Goldmine of Games*. Fort Atkinson, Wis.: Alleyside Press, 2000.

Simon, Charnan. *Librarians*. Chanhassen, Minn.: Child's World, 2003.

On the Web

FactHound offers a safe, fun way to find Web sites related to this book. All of the sites on FactHound have been researched by our staff. *www.facthound.com*

1. Visit the FactHound home page.
2. Enter a search word related to this book, or type in this special code: 1404811508.
3. Click on the FETCH IT button.

Your trusty FactHound will fetch the best sites for you!